SIMPLE STRATEGIES FOR
MINDFULNESS

How to Slow Down, Reconnect with the
Important Things in Life, and Be Here Now

Nathalie Thompson

For information visit the author's web sites at:

www.NathalieThompson.com
www.VibeShifting.com.

ISBN: 978-0-9959942-2-5 (ebk)
ISBN: 978-0-9959942-3-2 (pbk)

Table of Contents

Introduction

To see a World in a grain of sand
And a Heaven in a wild flower
Hold Infinity in the palm of your hand
And Eternity in an hour
~William Blake

I was a teenager when I first read William Blake's poem "Auguries of Innocence", the first lines of which are quoted above. I remember being completely entranced by these lines because, to me, they spoke of the power of perception; of being open to the magic that exists in the everyday world, if only we take the time to notice it.

Unfortunately, in the constant flurry of action that is modern life, this is a message that is all too easy to forget. We live in a world that exhorts us to hustle harder, go faster, do more and be better than everyone else. But to what end and at what cost? In buying into the prevailing belief that "success" means having fancier cars, a bigger house, flashier toys, and more exotic vacations than other people, we completely lose touch with the things that actually matter in life.

Life is in the Moments

Our lives are made up of individual, irreplaceable moments, but most of us are rushing through those moments so quickly that we never even notice them. This book is about stepping out of that frenzied rush and finding our way back to the wonder of just being alive in this extraordinary world we all live in.

When was the last time you just sat and enjoyed being in the moment without worrying, multi-tasking, or thinking about anything other than what you were doing in that moment? Can you even remember a time when you were content to just sit and be who you were, doing what you were doing, without wishing you were somewhere else, or that your life was any different? When was the last time you lay in the grass and watched the clouds or actually stopped to look at the pebbles your kids brought to you in excitement, without dismissing them with a preoccupied "That's nice, sweetie," and not even looking at the treasures offered in those tiny hands?

An Auto-Pilot Existence

When we spend our days thinking about other things — wishing we were *there* rather than fully experiencing what it's like to be *here*, in other words — we end up going through our days on autopilot without fully experiencing them.

Don't believe me? Ask yourself how much of your life you actually live versus how much of it you just ignore. Can you answer any of the following questions?

- What was your child or your partner talking about this morning?
- Did you enjoy the lunch you ate two days ago?
- What colour are your best friend's eyes?

Most people will have a hard time answering these questions without having to stop and really think about it - if they can answer them at all.

Now, none of that is earth-shaking stuff, perhaps. But it's just a tiny fraction of the moments of our lives that we completely miss every single day. Most of us go through our entire adult lives focused on the future (thinking about groceries we need to pick up, what's on our "to do" lists, what time our kids need to be dropped off or picked up, what's on our calendar tomorrow, etc.) or on the past (worrying whether something we said in a meeting yesterday made us look stupid, or what

3

somebody else really meant when they said or did something last week, etc.) As a result, we are never really aware of what's happening right now – we're not really *living* our lives. We are going through the motions but we have stopped *experiencing*.

Alive But Not Living

The consequences of these half-lives that we lead are enormous. We live in a world of ever-increasing mental health issues and stress-related illnesses. We are more digitally connected than ever before, but increasing numbers of us feel isolated and alone. The tools that were supposed to reduce our workload, or at least make it easier, now ensure that we never really leave work behind when we walk out of the office, so even when we're "off", we're still working. In a fully connected world, it's always business hours somewhere and we feel guilty if we're not ensuring our customers six time-zones away can still reach us during their daytime, even when it's our nighttime.

In effect, we've lost our ability to turn off the outside world and give ourselves the time we need to fully relax and recuperate without worrying about things that (we believe) still need to get done. And the cost of this is high; without regular downtime to regenerate ourselves on both a mental and physical level, we start to break down.

To put it another way: just as a field needs time to rest without "working" if it is to produce at capacity, our minds and bodies must also rest in between periods of production and activity. Without this regular "fallow" time, we can't properly renew our internal resources. And it's making us increasingly exhausted, sick, frustrated, and despondent.

A Growing Movement

There is a growing movement afoot in the world, however, calling for us to return to a simpler, healthier way of life. It's a movement that asks us to start taking the time to both notice and appreciate the present, as it happens. It's a philosophy that asks us to understand that all we ever really have in life is this one present moment of NOW; it asks us to accept the fact that the past is gone and the future is never guaranteed, therefore, when we obsess over them we waste the precious gift that is right now.

This is a movement about *mindfulness*, or more accurately, *mindful awareness* of the moments of our lives.

How this Book Will Help You

In this book we're going to go over some simple, easy-to-implement mindfulness techniques that you can use, in whatever little pockets of time you can find within your day, to help you reap all the wonderful benefits of becoming more mindfully aware.

By the time you've finished this book you will be able to use any of the thirty mindfulness techniques presented herein to:

- Feel calmer and more in control of your life;
- Feel more satisfied with your personal relationships, and even your job;
- Shift from mindlessly *doing* your life to actively *being in* your life

In short, learning how to be mindful will help you feel happier with your life and with the world at large. And what's the cost of reaping all of these benefits? Nothing more than a few minutes of your time, whenever you can find them during your day.

Practicing mindfulness is something you'll have to consciously think about doing at the beginning, but over time it will simply become a part of who you are. You won't have to "practice" mindfulness anymore, you will simple *become* mindful.

If you're ready to make that shift, then let's continue...

Chapter 1:
What is Mindfulness?

IF YOU ARE DEPRESSED,
YOU ARE LIVING IN THE PAST.
IF YOU ARE ANXIOUS,
YOU ARE LIVING IN THE FUTURE.
IF YOU ARE AT PEACE,
YOU ARE LIVING IN THE PRESENT.
~LAO TZU

In this chapter we're going to define mindfulness so that it becomes easier for you to integrate it into your life. Knowing the how and the why behind a new concept often makes it easier for your mind to accept and incorporate it into your existing view of the world.

The problem at the moment, however, is that mindfulness has become one of those popularized buzzwords that people throw around without fully understanding; it has become a fuzzy concept that everyone talks about but no one really knows the meaning of. There are a lot of conflicting definitions out there, which can make it seem intimidating for those who might be considering mindfulness as a means of improving the quality of their own lives.

Common Mindfulness Myths

So let's begin our definition of mindfulness by clearing up a few common misunderstandings. There are three main myths about mindfulness that you may have come across online:

1. Mindfulness in just another word for meditation.

2. Mindfulness is difficult and time-consuming.

3. Mindfulness is fluffy New-Age nonsense.

Let's take a look at each of these myths in turn so that you can start your mindfulness journey with a clear understanding of what is – and what isn't – involved.

Myth #1:
Mindfulness is Another Word for Meditation

While there are many meditation practices that can help you cultivate mindfulness, it's important to understand that the two concepts are not interchangeable.

The critical distinction is that meditation is something that you *do*, while mindfulness is something that you *are*. Mindfulness, in other words is a state of being.

When we meditate, we work at silencing the "monkey mind" – all the self-talk, judgements, and commentary that run through our heads most of the time. When we are being mindful, we are simply allowing ourselves to fully experience our lives as they are happening. And this is important because life, as I said before, only really happens in the moments.

Mindfulness is being present and aware in each of those moments rather than just passing through and not even noticing them because we are thinking about other things, or because we are barrelling through them while panicking about things that are already in the past or which haven't even happened yet (and may, in fact, never happen).

Myth #2:
Mindfulness is Difficult and Time-Consuming

Nothing could be further from the truth than this particular mindfulness myth! The whole point of mindfulness is to be present and aware *in the moment*. It isn't supposed to be something that gets added to your already crazy "to do" list, and certainly isn't something that will add to your stress level. On the contrary, mindfulness is likely to reduce your stress level because it has the effect of slowing down your racing thoughts and letting you experience your life as something other than the barely-in-control race car careening down a hill that so many of us feel our lives have become.

While therapeutic courses in mindfulness generally take eight weeks of formal training, mindfulness, at its heart, is simply about reclaiming moments of full awareness and serenity in our otherwise hectic lives.

Myth #3:
Mindfulness is Fluffy New-Age Nonsense

In Chapter 2 you'll learn that, far from being New-Age nonsense, the wide-ranging benefits of mindfulness are consistently being proven in recent scientific studies.

From its use with patients suffering from clinical depression, to its ability to improve people's general job satisfaction and happiness in personal relationships, to the studies that show it improves brain density and function, mindfulness is truly a phenomenon that can help you improve your quality of life quickly, easily, and without any additional burden to your family budget.

Core Components of Mindfulness

So, now that we've dispelled the most common mindfulness myths, we are getting much closer to understanding the true nature of mindfulness. In order to really "get" it however, we need to better understand its three core components: present-moment awareness, self-awareness, and non-judgment.

Core Component #1:
Present-Moment Awareness

At its heart, mindfulness is the practice of consciously and deliberately focusing on the present moment rather than worrying about what *could* happen in the future or regretting what happened in the past.

We spend so much of our time obsessing about what may never happen and what is already over, but to what end? Any scenario we dream up about the future, whether we imagine it to be positive or negative, is only hypothetical. And no amount of self-recrimination is going to change what happened or what didn't happen in the past.

This doesn't mean that we don't plan for or prepare for the future, of course, but it does mean that we stop *worrying* about it. We come to understand that the only moment over which we have any control at all is what happens in the now. Our power lies in the present moment; always and only.

Core Component #2:
Self-Awareness

The second core component of mindfulness is becoming consciously aware of yourself on a mental, physical, and emotional level. And while this component does tie in with present-moment awareness in some ways, it's important enough to warrant its own category.

Another growing buzzword in the pop psychology field right now is "self-care", and that's because it's so important. But in order to take care of yourself, you need to become *aware* of what it is that you need. In our very busy modern lives we are constantly on the go and always plugged into one device or another. As a result, we rarely take the time anymore to check in with ourselves and see how we're doing.

So many of us have this nagging feeling that something isn't quite right, but we can't quite explain – to ourselves or anyone else – what it is that's wrong because we don't *know* what's wrong. We no longer know what we think or what we feel. And we no longer have any real connection with or awareness of the current state of our own bodies.

Core Component #3:
Non-Judgment

There is one other core component of mindfulness, and that is the idea of experiencing life without judging it. This involves becoming aware of our thoughts and feelings and accepting them without labelling them either "bad" or "good".

We have a tendency to think of our emotions as being either positive or negative, but in reality they are neither. Yes, there may be some that we prefer to feel over others, but in and of themselves, our emotions – all of them – are equally valid and valuable to us. Both the emotions we like to feel (what we call the "good" ones) and the ones we don't like to feel (what we call the "bad" ones) are part of our emotional guidance system, and they all provide us with important information about where our *thoughts* are focused.

We have tens of thousands of thoughts every day, too many to ever be consciously aware of. Which means – and this is the critical point here – they are always changing. Mindfulness helps us to understand the fleeting, flowing nature of our thoughts and feelings so that we can learn not to get caught up in them or to let ourselves be defined by them. However pleasant or unpleasant a thought or feeling we are currently having might be, when we look again only moments later they will have already changed.

This ability to observe our own thoughts and feelings as we're experiencing them, and to interpret them as mental events rather than the objective reality of the situation, is known as *metacognition* and it's one of the key traits that allows you to maintain perspective on the events of your life and to respond to them with intention rather than blindly reacting to them.

Mindfulness Defined

Now that we've dispelled the three main mindfulness myths and learned the three core components of mindfulness, it's time to tie everything together with a clear definition of the term:

Mindfulness is the state of becoming fully and deliberately aware of the present moment. This involves awareness and acceptance of our thoughts, feelings, and physical sensations without criticism or judgment.

In short, mindfulness is about putting an end to our habit of living life on autopilot. Instead of going through our days like automatons being pushed through our actions and behaviours by subconscious programs and habits that we no longer even think about or question, we simply become aware of our lives and our experiences as they are, in the moment in which we are.

Chapter 2:
Why Mindfulness?

YOU PRACTICE MINDFULNESS, ON THE ONE HAND,
TO BE CALM AND PEACEFUL. ON THE OTHER HAND,
AS YOU PRACTICE MINDFULNESS AND LIVE
A LIFE OF PEACE, YOU INSPIRE HOPE
FOR A FUTURE OF PEACE.
~ THÍCH NHẤT HẠNH

There are many physical and psychological benefits of mindfulness. Anecdotal evidence abounds telling us that the use of mindfulness can help decrease stress levels, which, in turn, leads to improved mental and physical health. And all over the internet there are countless articles in which people consistently say that mindfulness helps to reduce insomnia, improve concentration, and increase feelings of overall peacefulness.

Such personal stories are always interesting, of course, but they never constitute *proof* that something actually works. If there is even an ounce of scepticism in you, you're probably asking yourself if there's any *real* evidence that all this mindfulness stuff is worth it. And rightly so! No matter where you hear something, it is always wise to ask questions, especially where claims are being made about human health or well-being.

In the case of mindfulness, fortunately, there is a great deal of scientific research telling us that it does have immense benefits and really can help us improve our lives.

Mindfulness and Mental Health

In the field of clinical psychology, numerous studies have been done, and continue to be done, investigating the role mindfulness can play in helping people live their lives with less anxiety, stress, and depression. There are even entire therapeutic systems that are based, at least partially, on mindfulness principles.

For example, Mindfulness Based Cognitive Therapy (MBCT) is kind of psychotherapy that uses both mindfulness practices and cognitive behavioural therapy to help people become aware of their automated thoughts and feelings, without associating *themselves* with those thoughts and feelings. In other words, it helps people to understand that the thoughts and feelings they have are ever-changing things that pass through the mind, rather than fixed personal traits that are inherently a part of who they *are*. This approach has been shown to significantly reduce the recurrence of depression in individuals with multiple previous episodes of major depressive disorder.[1]

Mindfulness and Work

Outside of clinical settings, mindfulness has also been shown to have additional benefits in the work world where it has been show to both increase job satisfaction and significantly lower emotional exhaustion.[2]

Other studies have shown that mindfulness training decreases rumination and increases both working memory and the ability to pay attention to things.[3] When we're not obsessing about all the things we hate or think are unfair about our jobs, we are free to simply do the work we are there to do, as best as we are able.

Mindfulness and Relationships

In the realm of our personal lives, several studies have shown that an increase in mindfulness in individuals involved in relationships increases the level of satisfaction that both individuals feel about the relationship.[4][5]

The research suggests that a person's ability to be mindful can help improve relationship satisfaction because it increases the ability to cope with the stress of any conflicts within the relationship and improves the ability to both recognize and communicate one's own emotions to a partner. This is helpful not just in romantic situations, but in all other forms of human interpersonal relationships, as well.

Mindfulness and Your Brain

Beyond the benefits to human psychological wellbeing, researchers are even starting to see that mindfulness causes physical changes and improvements within the brain itself [6]; a 2013 study by researchers from Carnegie Mellon and the University of Pittsburgh, for example, found that after only eight weeks of mindfulness training the amygdala (the brain's fight or flight response centre) became smaller.[7] Another study, by researchers affiliated with Harvard University found that MRIs of research subjects showed increased density in grey matter in several areas of the brain involved in learning and memory processes, emotion regulation, and perspective taking, again after only eight weeks of a mindfulness-based stress-reduction program.[8]

What these findings imply is that, as you become more mindful, the more primitive parts of your brain that deal with fear and stress become weaker, and the parts of your brain that deal with higher-order functions like awareness, emotions, concentration, and decision-making become stronger.

Beyond its applications with stress reduction and increased concentration, there are even some studies indicating that mindfulness may increase immune function[9] and help lower the risk of Alzheimer's disease.[10] With an aging population, this could have dramatic effects on the lives of millions of people around the world, at no cost to afflicted individuals, their families, or even their health insurance companies.

All of the Ups and None of the Downs

What all this research shows us is that mindfulness has many potential benefits for our health and well-being. At the very least, it's worth giving it a try; with so much that could be gained and nothing to lose but our worry, stress, and anxiety, mindfulness is a free and easy way to a more peaceful, content, and possibly even healthier life experience.

Chapter 3:
How to Practice Mindfulness

WHAT WOULD IT BE LIKE IF I COULD ACCEPT LIFE –
ACCEPT THIS MOMENT – EXACTLY AS IT IS?
~TARA BRACH

So you've decided that, with all the upsides to mindfulness, you're ready to give it a try. But where do you begin? Is it going to take up a lot of your already limited free time? Not at all! Research indicates that even brief training in mindfulness can reduce fatigue and anxiety and improve both your mood and your ability to concentrate.[11]

The most important thing to realize is that it doesn't have to be complicated. Mindfulness is meant to help you – not make your life more stressful. In other words, if sitting in lotus position and meditating for half an hour at a time doesn't appeal to you, then find something else, instead! Mindfulness, as you learned in Chapter 1, does not have to involve traditional meditation techniques.

The nice thing about mindfulness is that it really is as simple as *choosing* what you're going to focus on at any given time. It doesn't require any special tools or training. You just need to find ways to stop and notice what's happening in your life right now, until that noticing becomes your usual habit.

Keep it Simple

The best way of creating that "habit of noticing" is to start using simple little techniques that you actually enjoy doing, and which "fit" with both your lifestyle and your personality. And this book is designed to give you that kind of training in the form of fun and easy games that you're going to *want* to play. That way you'll start building up a habit of being mindful, without even realizing that's what you're doing.

In the following chapters you'll learn a number of quick mindfulness games that you can use to start bringing more mindfulness into your life, without all the hassle, guilt, and structure of trying to implement a standard meditation practice.

In Chapter 4 you'll find twenty single-player mindfulness games – simple little exercises that you can do on your own whenever you want to take a little mindfulness break. In Chapter 5 you'll find ten multi-player group mindfulness games for those times when you'd like company with your mindfulness practice, or when you'd like to introduce the concept to your family, friends, or colleagues in an entertaining way. (These games, incidentally, make great team-building exercises or icebreakers that you can use during corporate retreats.)

Being and Doing

In Chapter 1 you learned that mindfulness is something that you *be* rather than something that you *do*. You may be wondering, then, why the mindfulness games in this book are presented as things to do. I've done this deliberately so that you can start to get a feel for how *you* feel when are in that mindfulness zone of being.

The games in the following chapters are meant to be quick and easy ways of getting you into that zone so that you can experience yourself in mindful awareness of the present moment. As you gain experience with these games and become more comfortable with getting into that mindful state, you'll find that you start to slip into it at other times during your day without even trying.

In other words, the more you practice these games the stronger your "mindfulness muscles" will become, the quicker you will build a *habit of mindfulness*, and the greater the beneficial impact it will have on your life. If you continue playing these games regularly, you will notice fairly quickly that you are automatically more mindful without having to think about it. This is how you will know that you're making that shift from *doing* to *being* that I mentioned in the introduction to this book.

Chapter 4:
Single-Player Mindfulness Games

IN THIS MOMENT,
THERE IS PLENTY OF TIME.
IN THIS MOMENT,
YOU ARE PRECISELY AS YOU SHOULD BE.
IN THIS MOMENT,
THERE IS INFINITE POSSIBILITY.
~VICTORIA MORAN

In this chapter, you'll find twenty simple mindfulness games that you can do by yourself. Remember, this is not something that has to take up a lot of time before you start seeing the benefits. Even a minute or two a day, just enough time to play one of these games, is enough for you to start feeling the difference that mindfulness can make in your mindset and feelings of well-being.

You will notice that some of these games have an "Ante-Up" version that you can try if you'd prefer something that takes little more concentration than the basic game. You can either start with the classic game, or you can go ahead and dive right into the deep end with the greater challenge.

Game 1:
See Your Breath

Breathing exercises have always been popular means of increasing mindfulness. Breath is life. And focusing ourselves on our breathing is an excellent way to connect with life in the present moment. If you can find just two uninterrupted minutes every day to sit in silence and focus on your breathing, it will help to reduce the feelings of tension and stress in your life

Close your eyes and breathe in. Imagine your breath coming in just a little ways and then as you breathe out, imagine it going outwards an equal distance. With each breath in, imagine the breath moving a little further into your body, and on each outward breath imagine it flowing an equal distance away from you. It may help to visualize your breathe as coloured vapour or mist, or something else easily visible.

Ante-Up: Dissolving Dis-Ease

Alternatively, you can imagine each inward breath being directed to each part of your body in sequence, starting from the top of your head down through your toes. As you see your breath reaching each specific body part, relax that body part as best you can. Imagine your in-breaths providing healing energy to your body. And as you breathe out, dissolve any tension, discomfort, or dis-ease you may be feeling, and let it all flow out of you with the exhale. (If you'd like help with this one, you can get a free copy of my stress relief guided meditation MP3 with the first book in this series, *Simple Strategies for Stress Relief.*)

Game 2:
Book Breathing

In this breathing exercise you'll be using music to relax your mind and allow you to focus fully on the way your body feels as you breathe.

Choose some music that relaxes you. I find instrumental pieces or songs in a language that you don't know work best for this one; that way you're not distracted by lyrics and thinking about them instead of the moment you're in!

Find a book that's heavy enough to feel, but not so heavy as to be uncomfortable. Lie down on your back somewhere comfortable, like a couch or your bed.

Stretch your legs out comfortably and let your arms and hands rest loosely at your sides. Place your book on your belly, wherever is most comfortable for you, then lie back, close your eyes, and just breathe. Focus completely on the sensation of the book rising and falling as you breathe and listen to the music.

Game 3:
Gifts From the Universe

One of the easiest things you can do to cultivate mindfulness is to just take a walk and pay attention to what's around you. Usually when we're walking, we're lost in thought, our minds on other things happening in our lives. But when you really pay attention to what's around you, you can have the most extraordinary experiences.

For example, I still remember one particular walk I went on, about a year ago. It had been cold and rainy for most of the week, but Saturday dawned clear and sunny and not too cold to enjoy the outdoors. So off I went for a walk. And it was wonderful to be outside again.

As I was walking, I began to take note of a number of little "surprises" along my route. I lost count of the number of woolly bear caterpillars I saw, a small sparrow sat on a fence post and sang to me, and I even saw two mice chase each other through the grass at the side of the path. I actually heard them squeak, which is what attracted my attention to them in the first place. It was like they went out of their way to be noticed by me.

I was so enchanted by the wildlife around me that day and I was flooded by this immense feeling of gratitude to be able to see and experience it. It was as if the Universe itself had gone out of its way to surprise and delight me by sprinkling tiny gifts all along the path for me to find.

So get outside and just... walk. Pay attention to how each step feels and the flow of your muscles as they move. Pay attention to what you hear, to the colours and shapes around you, and to the scents in the air. Avoid drifting off into thoughts about your schedule and task lists and just focus on what is happening right now, as you walk. And look for the little gifts the Universe has sprinkled along the way for you to find.

Game 4:
Lost in Colour

In this game, you get to lose yourself in the soothing effects of colour! Many people dismiss colouring as a child's pursuit, but there is a growing body of research backing up the anecdotal claims of adult colourists who insist that colouring helps to calm them down and reduce feelings of stress.

A 2017 study by researchers at the University of Chicago, for example, found a significant decrease in depressive symptoms and anxiety in women who coloured daily after only *one* week of colouring. [12] Those who scoff at colouring often claim that there is no creative aspect to colouring someone else's design, but some studies have shown that colouring pre-made designs results in greater states of flow than drawing.[13]

And while some studies have shown that colouring mandalas (complex patterns within circle shapes) results in greater reductions in anxiety and low-mood than colouring other shapes[14], it doesn't have to be that complicated. You can just pick up a kids' colouring book at the local dollar store, along with a pack of crayons and still get the benefits of getting lost colour.

Ante-Up: Add Complexity

If you prefer something more challenging than a children's colouring book, there are any number of adult colouring books available on the market now, including the two I created to help you unwind: *Mystical Mantras* and *Celtic Knots*.

And if even the more complex adult colouring books aren't enough to keep you focused on the present, here's an expert-level challenge for you: use your non-dominant hand when you colour!

Game 5:
Channeling Joy

Usually when we work with mindfulness exercises we focus completely on the here-and-now. With this particular game, however, we're actually going to draw on past emotions and channel them into our experience of the present.

Get yourself into a comfortable position, either lying down or sitting. Some people like straight backed chairs with their feet on the floor, but I prefer to sit cross-legged on a couch for this game. Do what feels most comfortable for you. Close your eyes and breathe slowly and deeply until you feel centred.

Now, think back to a time in your life when you felt completely joyful. What is the happiest memory that you have? Immerse yourself completely in that memory. What was happening? Where were you? Who were you with? Sit with that memory and then go deeper into the experience by engaging all of your senses: How did your body feel? What sounds, sights (colours, etc.) tastes and smells do you remember? Let all the sensations of the memory of joy fill you up. When you are ready, open your eyes and take this feeling with you into the rest of your day.

Game 6:
Daily Dishes

Mindfulness doesn't have to be something structured and planned. We can find ways to be mindful in simple, everyday activities like washing the dishes.

Instead of cursing the annoyance of having to deal with dishes every single day (as I frequently do), push those feelings aside and concentrate on what you're actually doing. Feel the heat of the water on your hands. Imagine you're a child doing this for the very first time and find joy in the bubbles from the dish soap and wonder in the iridescent colours on the surface of those bubbles. Enjoy the scent of the soap, and allow yourself to be soothed by the repetitive motions of washing and rinsing.

Game 7:
Voyage of the Apple

This game is about gratitude and awareness of the interconnectedness of life. You'll need an apple (or, if you don't like apples, pick some other fruit or vegetable that you do like to eat). Hold the apple in your hand and look at it. Note the colours and shape of this apple, and the patterning of its skin.

Think about where this apple came from and each step of the journey that it had to undertake before it came to you. Focus on gratitude for all who were involved in creating this apple and in bringing it to you:.

- Give thanks for worms in the soil that nourished the tree on which this apple grew.
- Give thanks for the bees that pollinated the apple blossoms.
- Give thanks for the sun and the rain that helped the apple grow.
- Give thanks for the farmer who tended the orchard that contained the tree.
- Give thanks for the workers who harvested and packed the apples from the orchard.
- Give thanks for the transport drivers who shuttled the boxes of apples from the farm to the store.
- Give thanks for the store owner who ordered apples from the farmer.
- Give thanks for the store employees who put the apples on the shelves.
- Give thanks to the person who went grocery shopping and brought this apple home to you.
- And finally, give thanks to the apple itself for the sustenance it is about to give you.

This is not just an apple you are about to eat, it is a constellation of life and energy, an intricate web of cause and effect that worked together seamlessly to become your snack. Marvel at this, because it really is a kind of miracle.

Game 8:
Five Senses Countdown

This is a mindfulness game that you can play anywhere, at any time. Stop what you're doing and look around you right now. Engage your five senses and make a note of:

- Five things you can see;
- Four things you can touch;
- Three things you can hear;
- Two things you can smell; and
- One thing you can taste (this can be a bite of food, a sip of something to drink, or just focus on the taste in your mouth right now).

This is a particularly good game if you find yourself slipping into a negative mindset during a daily commute, for example. Instead of stewing over how cramped and uncomfortable and late the bus is, distract yourself by focusing on your five senses!

Game 9:
Finger Massage

This is a good one if you find it easier to anchor yourself into the present moment when you have a physical sensation to focus on. There are also two ways in which this one can be done: using both hands or just one.

The Two-Hand Method

With the two-hand method, you want to start with the index finger and thumb of one hand placed on either side (either top-bottom or left-right) of the base of the thumb of the opposite hand. As you inhale, slide the "holding" finger and thumb to the tip of the "held" thumb, squeeze briefly as you reach the tip of thumb, and then, as you breathe out, slide back down to the base of the thumb. With your next breath, move onto the index finger, then the middle finger, then the ring finger, then the pinky finger, doing each one in turn. Then work your way back to the thumb. When you've massaged all the fingers on the first hand, you can switch over and do all the fingers on the other hand using the same process.

The One-Hand Method

If you're doing the one-hand method, it works much the same way, but you do it with just one hand. Put your thumb at the base of the index finger next to it (the same hand) and as you breathe in, run the thumb up to the tip of the index finger, squeeze finger and thumb together at the top, then run your thumb back down to the base of the index finger on your exhale. Again, do each finger in turn then work your way back to the index finger you started with.

This game helps you to breathe mindfully, focusing on your inhales and exhales, while simultaneously using the finger massage process to help you concentrate.

Game 10:
Stop and Smell the Roses

For this game, you'll need something with a strong scent, like a bouquet of roses. If you're not a fan of flowers, then use something like a small dish of coffee beans, a bottle of perfume, or a freshly cut lime. (Make sure you're using something scented but non-toxic. Don't do this with cleaning products or anything dangerous!)

Sit down at a table and place your scented object in front of you. Close your eyes and inhale deeply through your nose. Focus completely on the scent of the thing in front of you. As you inhale, pay close attention to what happens in your body as you smell this thing. Is there a physical sensation of any kind in your muscles, in your stomach, or inside your nose? Is your heart rate increasing or decreasing? Do you feel more alert or more relaxed? If it's a food item in front of you, is your mouth starting to water? What emotions or memories are evoked by this particular scent?

Game 11:
Abundance Awareness

For this one, all you need to do is look around you and realize that life is abundance exemplified. Abundance is everywhere and in everything that you see. Where there is grass, it's not just one blade of grass it is hundreds, thousands, millions of blades of grass. Likewise, when you look up at the sky, it's not just one star up there; there are – literally – too many to count.

If you live in a place where there is no grass and there are too many city lights to see the stars, then look around you and count the colours. Even in a cityscape full of concrete there are infinite shades of gray; there are shadows and pockets of light; there are people wearing every colour in the crayon box and more. If you scoop one single handful of sand out of a playground sandbox, there are more grains of sand than you could count (and that's just in *one* handful!)

And even within *you*, there is abundance! For example, there are as many breaths of air as you could want. You don't need to ask for them or think about them – they are just there when they are needed. And your own body is made up of more than thirty *trillion* cells that replicate and replenish themselves as needed.

Game 12:
Counting Colours

Similar to the abundance game above, counting colours is about noticing what's around you every single day that you just take for granted.

Stop what you're doing right now and look around you. Just in this one place where you are right now, how many colours can you see? Count them. Don't just list "green" or "blue" – go further than that. How many different shades or variations of blue can you see? When you look at trees or even a flat expanse of grass, it's not just "green" that you see; it is a riot of different shades and colours. Likewise, when you look at a field of freshly fallen snow it's not just white, it's endless variations of gray and yellow and pink and blue. When you stop assuming that you already know what's in front of you, you open your awareness and start seeing what's *really* there.

Game 13:
Showered in Mindfulness

One of the easiest ways to create a mindfulness habit is to be fully present while you're in the shower. Because it's something we do every day, the time we spend in the shower is a great way to get daily mindfulness practice in. But most of us jump into the shower and spend that time automatically going through the motions while thinking about the meetings we have scheduled, our upcoming dental appointment, the gift we still have to buy for the birthday party our child was invited to this weekend, and whether we need to stop and pick up more milk on the way home from work today.

In other words, our minds are on everything and anything except what we're doing. But what if we used the time in the shower to really be present? To let ourselves enjoy the feel of the water on our skin; to appreciate the scent of our shampoo; to observe the swirl of soap bubbles around our feet; to acknowledge and be truly grateful for the fact that our bodies work as well as they do, given the fact that most of us do not take as good care of them as we know we should!

Game 14:
Focus on the Flame

For this game, you will need a candle. Sit yourself comfortably in a chair with the candle on a table in front of you, or sit cross-legged on the floor in front of the candle. (Do not lie down for this game – you do not want to risk falling asleep with a candle burning!) You can leave the lights on if you want, but I prefer a dimly lit room for this exercise.

Light the candle and then focus on the flame. Really see it. Notice how the shape of it shifts, how any wisps of smoke curl up from it. Appreciate how the scent of it fills the air as the wax starts to melt. Focus all your senses on the candle. When other thoughts cross your mind, recognize that they are just thoughts, and then gently refocus yourself on the flame.

Game 15:
Observing Ants

All you have to do for this game is go outside, find a bunch of ants, and just watch them carefully for a few minutes. Don't expect anything, just observe what happens. See how the ants work together and what they're doing. If you have any food with you, try dropping a few crumbs near your ants and then watch them carry this treasure back to their nest.

I once watched an ant colony migrate. I don't know if they were moving the whole colony or if the colony had just gotten so big that they had to split into two groups, but there was a massive flow of them moving from one part of the lawn to another. They were even moving eggs. They didn't care that there was a "giant" watching them, they were so focused on what they were doing. It really was fascinating to watch.

If you can't find any conveniently located ants, you can use any large group of insects that you can find. On another occasion I just happened to be in the right place at the right time to catch a monarch butterfly migration. They were following a river through one of my country's national parks and I was walking along the beach next to a constant stream of beautiful, delicate orange creatures. There were more of them than I could count, and it was one of the most beautiful sights that I have ever seen.

Game 16:
Tuning In

So far, all our games have focused on physical sensations or visual awareness. With this game, we're going to focus on our sense of hearing. When we are in familiar surroundings, most of us tune out the background noises and don't even realize that they're there. This game is about overriding that automated tendency to mute the world around us and to, instead, deliberately focus on the ambient sounds of our environment.

Close your eyes and imagine that you are a radio that can tune in to different frequencies. Take a moment to just listen to the world around you. Now, focus on the sounds farthest away from you. What can you hear? Change the "station" you're on and focus closer, on the sounds in the room you're currently in. Change the station again and bring your focus even closer; concentrate on the sounds of *yourself* – your breathing, your heartbeat, you gurgling stomach, etc.

After you've listened to all three "stations", open your eyes. What was the hardest part of this game? What was the easiest? Were you distracted at any point? By what?

Game 17:
Window on the World

This is a game that you can do anywhere there happens to be a window, and it only takes a minute or two. Look out of the nearest window. Even if you've looked out of this particular window before, pretend that you are someone seeing this view for the first time. What do you see?

Try not to label things you see with words (i.e. "tree", "bird", "clouds", etc.) Focus instead on the colours, patterns, and movements of the things in your visual field. Do not criticize anything you see (e.g "The city really needs to fix that broken street light.") but just try to observe whatever is there without judgement.

Game 18:
Still Life Details

For this exercise you'll need some paper and either a drawing pencil or some pencil crayons.

Pick an ordinary object that you see every day in your environment, but which you never really think about, like a toothbrush or your morning coffee mug. The object you choose should be small and easily overlooked.

What I want you to do with it now is to *really* look at it. Take a minute to observe all the details of your object: the colours, the lines, the shadows, and the light. Really see this object as it is. Then what I want you to do is try to draw it! It doesn't have to be a masterpiece, the point here is to ground yourself in the moment by paying attention to all the details of something right in front of you, something that you come across every day but never think about and never really see.

Ante-Up: Still Life From Memory

If you want to challenge yourself with this one you can cover the object with a towel, after you've taken a minute to observe the details, and then draw it from memory.

Game 19:
Deep Thoughts

If you find it hard to focus on the present because your mind is always racing with thoughts, then this game may appeal to you because you're giving your busy mind exactly what it wants: something to think about. The sneaky part is that, rather than letting it run rampant with to-dos and what-ifs, you guide it to think about something specific.

You'll need a book that is meaningful to you or a deck of oracle cards or something similar. (You're looking for something that has many discrete elements or self-contained sections in it, like a collection of individual poems.)

One of the books that I like to use for this game is the *Tao Te Ching*. I find it extremely useful as a kind of meditative tool, as there are so many layers of meaning within each of the teachings therein. I like to open the book at random, read the verse that appears, and then take some time to think about what it means.

When you immerse yourself completely in the verses of the *Tao Te Ching* (or any other material you feel connected to), you allow yourself to still the runaway voices and endless task lists running through your head and focus on one thing alone. You become mindful of that which is in front of you and let everything else go, if only for a few minutes.

Game 20:
A Moment of Gratitude

This is a particularly good game when you're having one of those days where absolutely everything seems to be going wrong. When a chain reaction of negativity gets started, it's so easy to get sucked into a "woe is me" mind frame where we start to think the entire Universe is out to get us. And the longer we stay in that kind of mindset, the harder it is to get out of it, and the more we focus on everything else that's going wrong in our lives.

The moment of gratitude has the effect of hitting the pause button on those runaway negative thoughts by refocusing your attention on something else before the snowball of doom gets too big.

What you do is stop everything. Take three very deep and slow breaths, in and out. And then say "Despite all that is happening, right now I am grateful for [whatever you're currently grateful for]." It doesn't have to be something earth-shakingly big; it just has to be something that you are honestly grateful for.

For example, you might say: "Despite all that is happening, right now I am grateful for the fact that my children are healthy and happy." Or "Despite all that is happening, I am grateful for the flock of sparrows that came to my feeder today." Or "Despite all that is happening, I am grateful to have a roof over my head and friends who love me."

Chapter 5:
Multi-Player Mindfulness Games

WHEN WE GET TOO CAUGHT UP
IN THE BUSYNESS OF THE WORLD,
WE LOSE CONNECTION WITH ONE ANOTHER –
AND OURSELVES.
~JACK KORNFIELD

Sometimes you just want to focus on your own mindfulness practice, but it's actually a lot of fun when you play with a group! This chapter provides ten multi-player games that you can use to practice mindfulness with friends, family, co-workers, or other groups.

As with the single-player games you learned in Chapter 4, group mindfulness games will help you strengthen your mindfulness "muscles". They have an added benefit, however, that single-player games do not: multi-player mindfulness games can also help you strengthen your human connection to others.

This additional human element is important. In his book *Flourish*, psychologist Dr. Martin Seligman says that positive human connection is one of five pillars to human well-being, and that "Other people are the best antidote to the downs of life and the single most reliable up."[15] When we are mindful with the people who matter to us, the benefits for all are even greater than with mindfulness alone!

Game 1:
Tangled Web

You'll need at least six people for this game to work. The bigger the group, the better (and more complex) it gets. You'll also need a ball of yarn.

Everyone needs to stand in a circle and the person with the ball of yarn grabs hold of the end of the yarn and passes the ball to someone else. The ball is passed to each group member only once, criss-crossing the circle and unravelling as it goes. Each person who receives the ball needs to keep hold of a section of the yarn as they pass the ball on.

Pay careful attention to the order in which the ball gets passed around because once the ball has been passed to everyone and all group members are holding onto a section of yarn, it's time to wind it all back up by passing the remaining yarn ball back around in the opposite order from which it sent out. Be careful not to let the web get tangled or let the ball drop!

Ante-Up: Double Trouble

If you'd like an extra challenge, add a second ball of yarn to the mix, so that everyone is holding a piece of both balls, and you have to rewind both balls without getting them tangled with themselves or each other.

Game 2:
Coin Connection

In this game, you'll need a bowl with enough of the same kind of coin for every person who is playing. Pennies work well, but whatever you've got enough of is fine.

Each person reaches into the bowl and pulls out a coin. Set a timer for one minute and have everyone study their coin carefully in order to create a connection with it. You each want to really get to know your own coin and all its unique quirks.

When the timer goes off, have everyone put their coin back into the bowl. Shake up the coins and then tip them out onto a table or the floor. Taking it in turns, everyone has to find their own coin and then explain how they know it's their own coin.

Game 3:
Keep Your Balance

Begin this game by asking all players to stand in a circle. Then have everyone stand on one leg and see who can hold the position longest without losing balance.

Ante-Up: Be the Tree

To add a level of challenge to this game, turn your knee outward and bring your raised foot in behind your standing-leg knee, like a sideways flamingo. Bring your hands together in a prayer position in front of your heart (this is the classic yoga "Tree Pose") then slowly raise your hands to form a mountain peak over your head.

For an even greater challenge, from the above pose, while keeping your arms over your head, pull your hands apart into a Y. If you're still balancing, try leaning your whole upper body forward while stretching your raised leg out straight behind you so that you'd look like a letter "T" from the side.

If you've managed to get through all levels of this game, then try the entire sequence again while standing on your other leg!

Game 4:
Don't Lose Your Marbles

For this game you'll need a small bowl filled with marbles, and one spoon for each group member. With everyone sitting at a table, the object of the game is to see who can balance a marble on their spoon the longest without dropping it.

Ante-Up: Marbles on the Move

If you want to add to the challenge, have everyone pass their spoon to the person on the right without anyone losing their marbles.

For an even greater challenge, try walking around the table while balancing your marbles on your spoons, or create a relay from one side of the room to the other, passing one marble from spoon to spoon across the length of the room.

Game 5:
Sketch Artist

This is a game for two or more players. One player will be the narrator and all other players will be sketch artists. Each sketch artist will need a blank piece of paper, a blindfold, and a pencil. If you don't have enough room for everyone to sit at a table, you will also need clipboards for each sketch artist to draw on.

Once everyone is comfortably seated, all sketch artists must put their blindfolds on. The narrator's job at this point is to describe a simple scene or an imaginary individual, while the sketch artists listen mindfully for each detail. When the narrator has finished his or her description, the sketch artists are given three minutes to use their pencils and paper to draw the described scene or person without looking at what they are drawing. When the sketch time is up, all players can remove their blindfolds and share their masterpieces with the group.

Game 6: Bean Bag Blitz

This is a classic don't-drop-the-ball catch game with a twist. You'll need at least five people, as well as a bunch of bean bags or stuffed animals (any soft smallish things are fine).

Have everyone stand in a circle then toss a bean bag to another player. That person then tosses it to someone else, as you toss a second bean bag to another player in the circle. Now there are two bean bags being tossed around the circle. Add another bean bag. Then another. Then another. Keep adding bean bags until all of them are in play, being tossed around the circle. Everyone has to be alert and mindful of who they're tossing to and who's tossing to them so that none of the bean bags get dropped.

Game 7:
Two Lies and a Truth

This is a game for five to ten people that I learned through Toastmasters.

Taking it in turns, each person in the group will stand up and tell the group three things about him or herself. Two of the things must be lies and one must be a truth, and these can be told in any order the speaker wishes to tell them (truth-lie-lie or lie-lie-truth or lie-truth-lie).

The other group members try to figure out, by carefully listening to and observing the speaker, which one of the statements or stories is the truth. Each group member gets a turn to explain which story they think is the true one, and, more importantly, *why* they think it was the truth, based on their mindful listening and observations.

Game 8:
Gratitude Chain

This game can be played in one of two ways. If you have a group of people who all know each other fairly well, you can do a name chain where player one states something for which they are grateful about another player, and why. That player then says what they're grateful for about a third player, who then continues the chain by saying what they're grateful for about yet another player, until everyone has had a turn.

For example: Player one says: "I am grateful for Mary's laugh because it's the kind of laugh that makes everyone else laugh, too." Then Mary says: "I am grateful for Joe's help in critiquing my novel – his insight helped me make the manuscript so much better". Then Joe says "I am grateful for Bob's help with setting up the room for our meeting today because together we got the place ready in record time", etc.

If you've got a group that's less familiar with each other, you can create your gratitude chain just by going around the circle in turn, with each player sharing what they are most grateful for today, and why.

Game 9:
Invisible Art

This is a game for two that I used to play with friends as a child. It should only be played by people who know each other well enough that physical contact would not be considered intrusive. In other words, this is not a game to play with work colleagues or in school settings – save it for close family or your "besties".

Sit cross-legged on the ground, one person in front, one behind. The person in front should rest comfortably with their eyes closed. The person behind uses his or finger as a pen to draw a picture on the front person's back.

The person being drawn on pays close attention to the sensations and tries to figure out what image is being drawn. Wait until the artist says the picture is finished to be sure you got the whole thing! Alternatively, you can try writing words instead of drawing pictures.

Game 10:
Digital Detox Dinner

Given our modern-day addiction to smart phones, this is the most challenging game in this book because I'm going to ask you to *turn the cell phone off* and reacquaint yourself with an unplugged, device-free way of life.

What you're going to do is invite a couple of friends over for dinner. It can either be a "prepare it together" party or you can handle all the cooking and prep yourself — just let your guests know upfront what you're planning. When everyone arrives, you all have to turn your cell phones off and put them into a basket which then gets shoved into a closet for the duration of the evening. That's right — you have to actually *talk* to each other. In person. With spoken words, not text messages!

But what if there's an emergency, you ask? How can anyone possibly survive without their phone for a whole evening? First off, we've completely lost perspective on what constitutes a real emergency these days. Not knowing the latest news the second it breaks on Twitter, for example, is not an emergency. Second of all, the odds of a real emergency cropping up in the few hours during which you'll be unavailable are statistically unlikely. Really.

Yes, you say – but what if there *is* a real emergency that happens during this time?

When I was a kid my house was gutted by a fire. We were out visiting friends at the time but, despite this having happened in those in those primitive times before cell phones had even been invented, the fire department had no problems tracking us down to get a hold of my father to let him know what was happening. Trust me on this – if there's ever a true emergency, the right people have ways of getting a hold of you.

So shut the cell phone off. Disconnect from email, from Twitter, from Facebook timelines and Snapchat stories. And just be in the moment with your guests. Enjoy their company. BE with them fully as you work together to prepare a meal and then enjoy it without the constant distraction of the digital world.

(Again, be upfront about your expectations when you invite people — make it clear that this is a one-evening digital detox and phone-checking will not be allowed. They can then either accept or decline according to the severity of their device addiction levels.)

Chapter 6:
Returning to Yourself

You are the sky.
Everything else is just the weather.
~Pema Chödrön

Congratulations, you've made it to the end of the book! At this point you now understand:

- What mindfulness is (and what it isn't);
- How mindfulness can improve your life, your health, and even your relationship and job satisfaction; and,
- How to use any of the thirty mindfulness games in this book to quickly and easily add mindfulness into your day.

The most important thing that you've learned, though, is that, while this book has provided a number of games to help you "do" mindfulness exercises, it's not about doing all or even any of those exercises. It's about what those exercises can help you cultivate within yourself. It's about slowing down and reconnecting with what's truly important to you by becoming more present in and aware of your life, in all of its moments.

Mindfulness is about finding that place inside of you where the real you, the You that cannot be touched by anything that happens in the outside world, resides. It's about coming back to your*self*.

You Are the Sky

So what does that mean? The more you work with these mindfulness games (and the Classic Mindfulness Meditation you will find later in this chapter), the more you will start to gain a clear awareness of the fact that there is a higher awareness — a greater You — that exists independently of your thoughts, observing them as they flow through you. This awareness, in turn, shifts your perception so that you come to understand that your thoughts and feelings are just things that happen in that greater field of awareness that is the real You.

To paraphrase Buddhist nun Pema Chödrön, you start to realize that you are like the sky, and everything else — your thoughts and feelings — are as variable as the weather that washes through without ever diminishing that sky. In other words, as you become mindful, you will begin to understand that you are more than your thoughts and more than your feelings. You may *have* thoughts and feelings, but those thoughts and feelings are not who you are.

The True Gift of Mindfulness

And this is the true gift of mindfulness: When you really start to understand this concept of the greater You, you're better able to cope with life's inevitable ups and downs because you *know* that any negative thoughts and feelings you have surrounding your situation do not define you.

This allows you to disentangle your sense of identity and self-worth from the conflicts and struggles of daily life. With the ability to know who you are outside of your thoughts and emotions, comes a greater perspective. You can assess the events of your life with greater objectivity because you are better able to "step out" of those situations and look at them without the clouding effects of your own feelings about them. You become less volatile, more resilient, and better able to chart your own course in life because you are no longer *reacting* to circumstance, but actively *responding* to it, instead.

What's Next?

Now that you've mastered the simple mindfulness games in this book, you may be wondering where to go from here. How can you take this way of being to the next level and really start to connect with the greater You?

My suggestion would be that you try a classic mindfulness meditation practice. The exercise below can be done for just a minute or two a day at first and then you can slowly build the time up until you can do it for longer periods (anywhere from five to thirty minutes at a time, whatever works best for you and your lifestyle).

Classic Mindfulness Meditation

Sit in a chair with your feet on the floor and your hands either in your lap or palm-down on your knees. Keep your spine straight and close your eyes.

Bring your attention to your body: the pressure of the chair against you, the sensation of your feet resting on the surface of the floor, the texture of the clothing underneath your hands, and the air entering and leaving your nose as you breathe. Stay focused on these sensations.

As thoughts flow through your mind, notice that they are thoughts, but gently bring your awareness back to your body. Observe your thoughts, but don't get caught up in them, and don't judge them. Try not to get frustrated with yourself when your attention wanders and the thoughts appear — it's expected that this will happen. Just bring your awareness back to your physical sensations over and over again, as often as you need to.

It will likely be difficult for you to stay focused with this exercise at first, even if you've mastered the other games in this book. But, as with all things, it will become easier with practice. Go easy on yourself, be forgiving of your fidgeting, and try again. As you continue with your practice you'll find that you're able to focus for longer periods.

There is Only Now

We live in a world defined by our collective avoidance of the present moment. We are afraid to stop and just be here now because we're afraid of what we'll find if we do. We fill our days with regrets about yesterday and worries about tomorrow and then, inevitably, we wonder what happened to our lives. We never seem to realize that our lives are lived solely in our *todays*.

If we are ever to fully experience our lives, we must reclaim our todays by breaking the cycle of avoidance that keeps us stuck in the past or in the future. And we do this by deliberately making it a point to pause during the otherwise swift pace of our days and simply notice ourselves and our experiences.

In changing our focus from always being somewhere else to being fully present right now, we allow ourselves to reconnect with the wisdom that has always lived within us, and we come to understand there is *only* right now. This moment is all we have, and all we are ever guaranteed. That makes it something special. And in becoming mindful of that, in deciding to truly *live* this one, precious moment as it happens, we find the clarity that returns us to ourselves.

A Letter to the Reader

Dear Reader,

I hope you enjoyed *Simple Strategies for Mindfulness*. Thank you so much for taking time out of your busy schedule to read it!

As you know, reviews are the lifeblood of any book – especially for us indie authors. Without them, our books quickly disappear from book store search algorithms and fade into obscurity. And that makes the books very, very sad.

If you'd like to help make this particular book very, very happy, it would be thrilled if you could leave it a review. You can do that right here:

(Just scan the QR code and then click the "Write a Customer Review" button at the bottom of the page).

Thanks so much, from both me and my book, and have a fantastic day!

Light and love,

Nathalie Thompson

Other Books By This Author

The Positive Affirmations Handbook
fearLESS

The Life Shifting Series:

Mind Shifting
Soul Shifting
Body Shifting (Coming Soon!)

The Simple Strategies Series:

Simple Strategies for Stress Relief
Simple Strategies for Mindfulness

Coloring Books:

Mystical Mantras Coloring Book
Celtic Knots Coloring Book

About the Author

Nathalie Thompson wants to live in a world where coffee pots are never empty and everyone is living the extraordinary life of their dreams.

A transformation catalyst and motivational expert, she is the author of *fearLESS* and *Mind Shifting* and her articles have been featured on the *Huffington Post* and on the blogs of NYT best-selling inspirational authors Pam Grout and Mike Dooley.

Connect with her and start transforming *your* dreams into reality over at www.VibeShifting.com!

/vibeshifting   @vibeshifting

References

[1] Teasdale, J., Segal, Z., Williams, J., Ridgeway, V., Soulsby, J., Lau, M. (2000) Prevention of relapse/ recurrence in major depression by mindfulness-based cognitive therapy. Journal of Consulting and Clinical Psychology, 68(4), 615-623.

[2] Hülsheger, U., Alberts, H., Feinholdt, A., Lang, J. (2013). Benefits of mindfulness at work: The role of mindfulness in emotion regulation, emotional exhaustion, and job satisfaction. Journal of Applied Psychology, 98(2), 310-325.

[3] Chambers, R., Lo, B., Allen, N.B. (2008) The Impact of Intensive Mindfulness Training on Attentional Control, Cognitive Style, and Affect. Cogn Ther Res 32: 303. https://doi.org/10.1007/s10608-007-9119-0

[4] Barnes, S., Brown, K., Krusemark, E., Campbell, W., Rogge, R. (2007), The role of mindfulness in romantic relationship satisfaction and responses to relationship stress. Journal of Marital and Family Therapy, 33: 482–500. doi:10.1111/j.1752-0606.2007.00033.x

[5] Khaddouma, A., Coop Gordon, K., Strand, E. (2017), Mindful Mates: A Pilot Study of the Relational Effects of Mindfulness-Based Stress Reduction on Participants and Their Partners. Fam. Proc., 56: 636–651. doi:10.1111/famp.12226

[6] Ireland, T. (2014). What Does Mindfulness Meditation Do to Your Brain. Retrieved from https://blogs.scientificamerican.com/guest-blog/what-does-mindfulness-meditation-do-to-your-brain/

[7] Taren A., Creswell J., Gianaros. P. (2013) Dispositional Mindfulness Co-Varies with Smaller Amygdala and Caudate Volumes in Community Adults. PLoS ONE 8(5): e64574. doi:10.1371/journal.pone.0064574

[8] McGreevery, S. (2011) Eight weeks to a better brain. Retrieved from https://news.harvard.edu/gazette/story/2011/01/eight-weeks-to-a-better-brain/

[9] Davidson, R., et al. (2003). Alterations in Brain and Immune Function Produced by Mindfulness Meditation. Psychosomatic medicine. 65. 564-70. 10.1097/01.PSY.0000077505.67574.E3.

[10] Larouche, E., Hudon, C., Goulet, S. (2015) Potential benefits of mindfulness-based interventions in mild cognitive impairment and Alzheimer's disease: an interdisciplinary perspective. Behavioural Brain Research, 276, pp. 199-212

[11] Zeidan, F., et al. (2010) Mindfulness meditation improves cognition: Evidence of brief mental training. Consciousness and Cognition doi:10.1016/j.concog.2010.03.014

[12] Flett, J., Lie, C., Riordan, B., Thompson, L., Conner, T., Hayne, H. (2017) Sharpen Your Pencils: Preliminary Evidence that Adult Coloring Reduces Depressive Symptoms and Anxiety. Creativity Research Journal Vol. 29 , Iss. 4

[13] Forkosh, J., Drake, J. (2017) Coloring Versus Drawing: Effects of Cognitive Demand on Mood Repair, Flow, and Enjoyment. Pages 75-82, Journal of the American Art Therapy Association, Vol. 34:02

[14] Babouchkina, A, Robbins, S. (2015) Reducing Negative Mood Through Mandala Creation: A Randomized Controlled Trial. Art Therapy Vol. 32 , Iss. 1

[15] Seligman, M. (2011). *Flourish: A Visionary New Understanding of Happiness and Well-Being.* Free Press. New York.

www.ingramcontent.com/pod-product-compliance
Lightning Source LLC
Chambersburg PA
CBHW031610040426
42452CB00006B/461

The Power of a Hurting Wife

McDougal & Associates

Servants of Christ and Stewards of the Mysteries of God

The Power of a

Hurting

Wife

Allison Davis

Unless otherwise noted, all scripture quotations are from the *Am-
plified Bible*, Copyright © 2015 by The Lockman Foundation, La
Habra, CA. References marked NKJV are from the *Holy
Bible, New King James Version,* copyright © 1979,
1980, 1982, 1990 by Thomas Nelson, Inc., Nashville,
Tennessee.

Published by:

McDougal & Associates
18896 Greenwell Springs Road
Greenwell Springs, LA 70739
www.thepublishedword.com

ISBN 978-1-940461-54-0

Printed on demand in the U.S., the U.K. and Australia
For worldwide distribution